mini ENCYCLOPEDIA

SEA

Contents

Life in the sea

Animals fill the sea and can be found all over the world around the seashore, in the shallows and in the very depths of the ocean.

Jellyfish

Jellyfish float in the sea. Many have long tentacles covered with poisonous stings.

Crustaceans

Crabs, lobsters and krill are all crustaceans.

Fish

There are many types of fish in the ocean. Sharks and rays are also fish.

Coral reefs

Coral reefs provide shelter and food for many fish and other sea creatures.

Marine mammals

Marine mammals
include whales, dolphins
and seals. Mammals give birth to live young
and feed their young with milk. They are
warm-blooded, which means their insides
stay warm even if it is cold around them.

Molluscs

Molluscs include octopuses,
squids, snails and clams.

Reptiles

Reptiles have scaly skin and
lay their eggs on land. Turtles
and sea snakes are reptiles.

5

Fish

Most fish belong to a group called bony
fish. Sharks, skates and rays belong to
a group called cartilaginous fish. Jawless
fish are another group of fish that include
only two types of fish.

Fins help the fish to
stay upright, tilt
and turn.

Many fish move
their tail to help
them push forward.

Bony fish

Bony fish have
a skeleton made
of bones. Most
bony fish also have
overlapping scales
covering their body.

Other bony fish

Moorish Idol   Swordfish   Clown Fish

Cartilaginous fish

Sharks, skates and rays have a skeleton that is made of cartilage. We have cartilage in our nose and ears. Instead of scales, cartilaginous fish are covered in tiny teeth called denticles.

A fish's gills are on the side of its head. When water passes over the gills, they take up oxygen so that the fish can "breathe".

Orangespine Unicornfish

Jawless fish

Lamprey

Hagfish and lampreys have lived in the ocean for millions of years. They are the only jawless fish still alive today. They do not have a jaw and their skeletons are made of cartilage.

Sea Horse

7

Fish life

To avoid becoming a meal for other sea creatures, some fish have developed special features and behaviour in order to survive.

Flying fish

Flying fish can jump out of the water to avoid predators. They spread out their side fins like wings to sail through the air – though they do not actually fly.

Sea horses

Sea horses can change colour in order to hide from their predators.

Some fish swim together in a large group called a school. They swim together at the same speed and in the same direction – almost like one giant fish. There can be thousands of fish in a school.

A shoal is another name for a group of fish. Shoals do not always swim at the same speed or in the same direction and can include fish of different types and sizes.

Sharks and rays

Sharks and rays have a skeleton made of cartilage, not bone. Cartilage is lighter and bendier than bone. It helps sharks and rays to stay afloat.

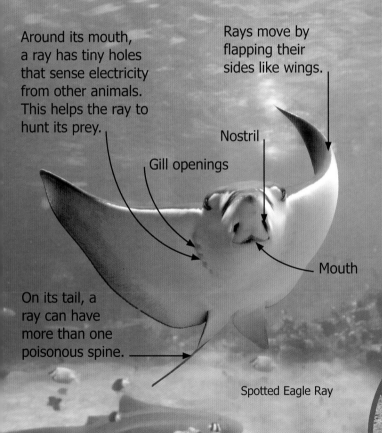

Around its mouth, a ray has tiny holes that sense electricity from other animals. This helps the ray to hunt its prey.

Rays move by flapping their sides like wings.

Nostril

Gill openings

Mouth

On its tail, a ray can have more than one poisonous spine.

Spotted Eagle Ray

Sharp, saw-like and pointed teeth help the Great White Shark to slice meat and bones.

The Great White Shark uses its gills to take oxygen from the water.

Pointed snout

A torpedo-shaped body makes it possible for the Great White Shark to swim quickly.

Fins help the shark to balance and swim.

Great White Shark

Keeping hidden

Stingrays hide by burying in the sand. This helps to protect them from predators like sharks and other rays.

Deep-sea fish

Some fish swim in the deepest depths of the ocean, where it is very cold and dark. This part of the ocean is home to a number of very strange fish. Scientists still have a lot to learn about many of these monsters of the deep.

Female Anglerfish

Female anglerfish are much larger than males.

Male Anglerfish

Attract and attach

Most anglerfish live in dark, deep waters, making it hard for them to find each other! When they mate, the small male attaches to the female's body. He can stay there for the rest of his life – even sharing her blood!

Lantern fish

Lantern fish have a pattern of lights along the side of their body. Scientists think this may help them to recognise each other in the dark depths.

Underside of lantern fish

Most anglerfish have a glowing light that hangs off their body like a fishing rod. They use the light to lure prey out of the darkness.

Anglerfish have a big mouth and a flexible body. This means they can swallow prey that is much bigger than they are.

Viper fish

The viper fish is another monster of the deep. It uses its huge teeth to grab its prey. Its teeth are so big, they don't fit inside its mouth.

Coral reefs

Coral reefs provide food and shelter for a huge variety of brightly coloured and unusual creatures. Although they look like plants, corals are actually related to jellyfish.

Some coral reefs get their bright colours from plants called algae, which grow within the coral reef.

How do coral reefs form?

An individual coral is usually very small and is called a polyp. The polyp attaches itself to a rock.

The polyp divides into more polyps.

Catching dinner

Corals use their tentacles to catch tiny animals to eat.

Seaweeds

Seaweeds are found on seashores and in shallow seas – including on coral reefs. Some seaweeds use a root-like anchor, called a holdfast, to attach themselves to a hard surface.

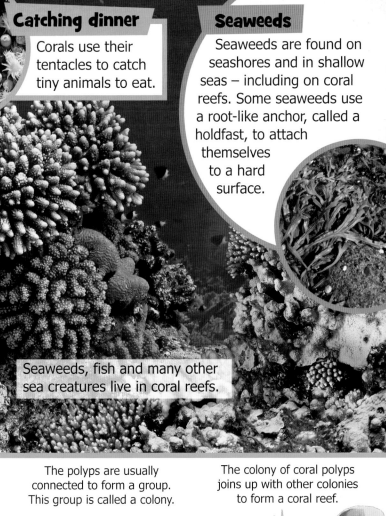

Seaweeds, fish and many other sea creatures live in coral reefs.

The polyps are usually connected to form a group. This group is called a colony.

The colony of coral polyps joins up with other colonies to form a coral reef.

Crabs

Crabs are crustaceans, which means they have a crust, or shell. True crabs have five pairs of legs, and two of their legs have claws on the end. Most crabs can move forwards slowly, but run quickly sideways. Some crabs move around by swimming.

Ghost Crab

Big and small

The largest crab is the Japanese spider crab! It can measure almost 4 m (13 ft) across when its legs are stretched out.

The smallest crabs are pea crabs – which can be smaller than the size of a pea!

When a crab gets too big, it splits open its shell and squeezes out. Its new shell can take up to three days to grow and harden.

Crabs' eyes are on stalks.

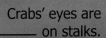

Hermit crabs do not have hard shells. So they find an old snail shell to live inside.

A crab uses its strong claws for show and for defence, but also for tearing apart food and cracking shells.

Crabs' gills are under their shell, near the top of each leg. They use them to take in oxygen.

A crab uses its back four legs to walk or run. If a crab loses a leg, a new one grows in its place.

17

Octopuses and squids

Octopuses and squids are both molluscs – like slugs and snails. They move by sucking water into their body and forcing it out again like a jet propeller. This action drives them quickly backwards through the water.

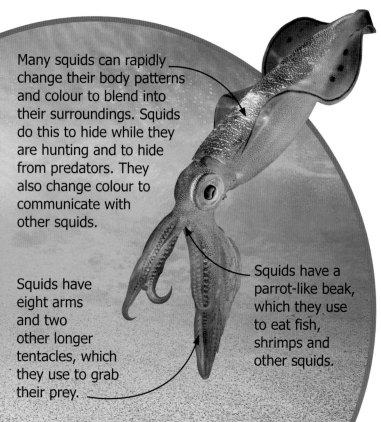

Many squids can rapidly change their body patterns and colour to blend into their surroundings. Squids do this to hide while they are hunting and to hide from predators. They also change colour to communicate with other squids.

Squids have eight arms and two other longer tentacles, which they use to grab their prey.

Squids have a parrot-like beak, which they use to eat fish, shrimps and other squids.

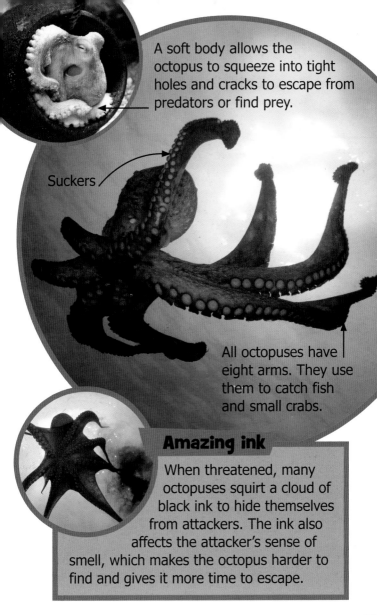

A soft body allows the octopus to squeeze into tight holes and cracks to escape from predators or find prey.

Suckers

All octopuses have eight arms. They use them to catch fish and small crabs.

Amazing ink

When threatened, many octopuses squirt a cloud of black ink to hide themselves from attackers. The ink also affects the attacker's sense of smell, which makes the octopus harder to find and gives it more time to escape.

Jellyfish

Jellyfish have simple, soft bodies that are made up almost entirely of water. They don't have bones, a brain or a heart! There are many different jellyfish – some can even glow in the dark.

Upside-down jellyfish

The cassiopeia jellyfish floats upside down and is also known as the upside-down jellyfish!

Other jellyfish

Moon Jellyfish   Irukandji Jellyfish   White-Spotted Jellyfish

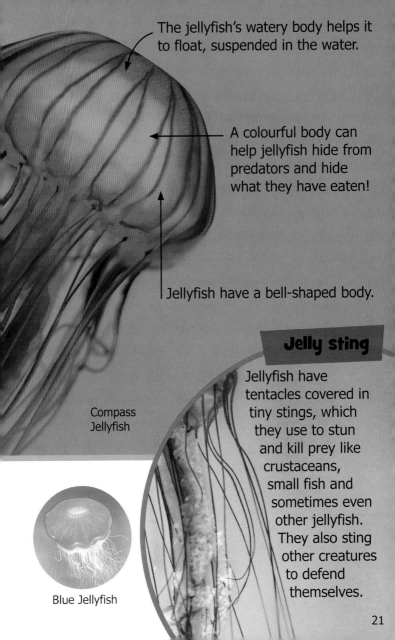

The jellyfish's watery body helps it to float, suspended in the water.

A colourful body can help jellyfish hide from predators and hide what they have eaten!

Jellyfish have a bell-shaped body.

Compass Jellyfish

Jelly sting

Jellyfish have tentacles covered in tiny stings, which they use to stun and kill prey like crustaceans, small fish and sometimes even other jellyfish. They also sting other creatures to defend themselves.

Blue Jellyfish

21

Whales

Whales are giant mammals. Millions of years ago, their relatives walked on land, but over time, their legs became flattened flippers and they moved into the sea. Whales can be divided into two groups: baleen whales and toothed whales.

Whales have a thick layer of fat beneath their skin. This keeps them warm in freezing oceans.

Eye

Baleen whales

The baleen is a fringe-like part found inside a baleen whale's mouth. It acts like a sieve to remove small animals from the water for the whale to eat. Baleen whales include the humpback whale and the blue whale.

Baleen

Breathing

Whales breathe in air through their blowhole, but unlike us they have to remember to breathe. Scientists think that they can let one half of their brain sleep, while the other half stays awake to breathe.

Whales swim by pushing their tail up and down.

Humpback Whale

Whales use their flippers to change their direction and position in the water.

Toothed whales

Sperm whales and dolphins are types of toothed whales. They all have teeth and only one blowhole.

Dolphins

Dolphins are playful and intelligent mammals. They belong to the toothed whale family, which includes killer whales and porpoises. They travel together in small groups called pods.

Dolphins breathe through their blowhole.

Melon

Pointed teeth help the dolphin to eat fish and squid.

Beak

Flipper

Echolocation

Dolphins "echolocate" to help them hunt and swim around obstacles. They make noises under the water that travel until they hit an object. The noises then bounces back as an echo to tell the dolphin the shape of the object and how far away it is. Dolphins use a fatty bulge on their forehead, called a melon, to echolocate.

A dolphin's sleek, long body helps it to be a speedy swimmer.

Killer whale

Killer whales are the largest animals in the dolphin family.

The dolphin's two tail flippers are called flukes. →

Dolphin acrobatics

Dolphins are excellent swimmers. They can also jump high out of the water. This is called breaching. The spinner dolphin gets its name from its extraordinary ability to leap and spin several times in the air.

Spinner Dolphin

Seals

Seals are mammals that live all around the world, including in the icy waters of Antarctica. Seals spend most of their time in the sea. They leave the sea to breed or to rest on land and on the ice.

Hindflippers

Foreflipper →

Fighting males

Most seals come on land in large groups in order to mate. Some male seals fight each other to prove who is the most powerful, and are often left with battle scars after a violent fight.

Male elephant seals fighting

Other seals

Monk Seal

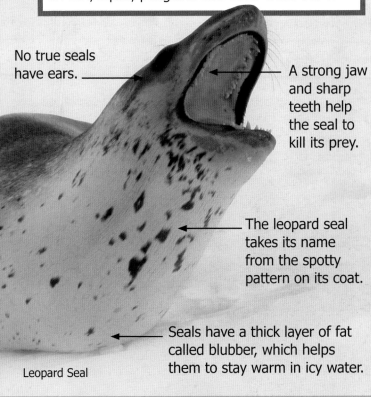

Leopard seals are powerful predators. They feed on fish, squid, penguins and other small seals.

No true seals have ears.

A strong jaw and sharp teeth help the seal to kill its prey.

The leopard seal takes its name from the spotty pattern on its coat.

Seals have a thick layer of fat called blubber, which helps them to stay warm in icy water.

Leopard Seal

Elephant Seal

Weddell Seal

Grey Seal

Sea turtles

Sea turtles are reptiles that can control the temperature of their body to survive in both cold and warm water. Sea turtles swim a long way in order to mate and find food. This journey is called migration.

The top part of the shell is called the carapace.

Most sea turtles' shells are made up of hard plates, which protect them from attackers like sharks.

Green Turtle

Other turtles

Loggerhead Turtle

Green Turtle

Leatherback Turtle

28

Sea turtles swim using four flipper-like legs. They are strong swimmers.

Sea turtles cannot pull their head fully back into their shell in the way that tortoises can.

The bottom part of the shell is called the plastron.

Dangerous nesting

Every few years, female sea turtles find a beach and lay their eggs. They dig a pit with their flippers, lay their eggs and cover the pit with sand. After about two months, young turtles hatch and head out into the sea. However, many are killed by predators before they can reach the sea.

Olive Ridley Turtle

Hawksbill Turtle

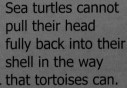

Glossary

This glossary explains some of the harder words in the book.

algae Like plants, algae are living things that make their food from sunlight. Algae do not have leaves, roots or stems and they mainly live in water.

baleen whale A type of whale that has sieve-like parts at the back of its mouth to sieve small animals out of the water.

beak A curved mouthpart found on turtles, squids, octopuses and birds.

cartilage A tough, material found in a human's ear, nose and joints. Cartilage forms the skeleton of sharks and rays.

claw A curved, sharp nail on an animal's foot.

colony A group of one kind of animal or plant that lives and works together.

defence The act of guarding or protecting something.

flipper A flat body part that some animals use for swimming.

gill A body part that allows fish and other animals that live in water to "breathe". Gills take in oxygen from the water.

oxygen A gas that all animals need in order to live.

predator An animal that hunts and eats other animals.

prey An animal that is hunted and eaten by another animal.

scales The small plates that overlap each other like roof tiles on an animal's body.

seashore An area of land that is at the edge of the ocean.

shallows A place where the water is not too deep.

shelter Something that protects from danger.

skeleton The bones and cartilage inside the body. The skeleton holds up the body and protects softer body parts.

snout The front part that sticks out from an animal's head. The snout includes the nose, mouth and jaws. A snout can also mean an animal's nose.

tentacle A long, thin body part. Animals use tentacles to feel or take hold of things.

toothed whale A type of whale that has teeth and a single blowhole.